T0209831

BiG, BAD POETRY

Biggest and Baddest in the west

BiG, BAD POETRY

Biggest and Baddest in the west

Sharon R. Leippi

BALBOA.
PRESS

A DIVISION OF HAY HOUSE

Balboa Press books may be ordered through booksellers or by contacting:

Balboa Press
A Division of Hay House
1663 Liberty Drive
Bloomington, IN 47403
www.balboapress.com
1 (877) 407-4847

Print information available on the last page.

ISBN: 978-1-9822-1694-8 (sc)
ISBN: 978-1-9822-1693-1 (e)

Balboa Press rev. date: 01/25/2019

Books by Sharon R. Leippi

Fire & Ice: ALASKA – Baked, Blended, & Sautéed
A gluten-free, dairy-free cookbook, also corn-free, with Alaskan photography from over thirty photographers.
(Frosty Books – 2012 – hard cover)

Think Hope Live: Embracing Life – Defeating Suicide
The focus is on suicide prevention.
Other topics covered: suicide alertness, and physician-assisted death.
(Balboa Press – 2017 – soft & hard cover and e-book)

Road Tripping from Alaska to New York City: Journaling the Journey & Taking Pix Along the Way
Traveling on the road with a pet, including photography and some history.
(Balboa Press – 2018 – soft cover and e-book)

Ubiquitous: Apple Juice, Lemon Juice, Olive Oil
A worldwide natural remedy of apple juice, lemon juice, and olive oil.
(Balboa Press – 2018 – soft cover and e-book)

Contents

V. Work

VI. Family

VII. Pets

Introduction

A "big and bad" joke on a scale of ten

Made us laugh, giggle, and feel good again.

    We couldn't be sad,

    We wouldn't feel mad,

The joke inspired a book to be written.

I. Geography

Heat Wave

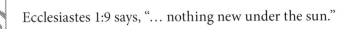

Ecclesiastes 1:9 says, "… nothing new under the sun."

Little lizard scurries into the shade,

Under red rock backdrop for a desert parade,

Past black widow spider and scorpion.

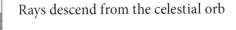

Rays descend from the celestial orb

Onto desert cacti and succulents,

Over roadrunner, coyote, rattling serpents,

And on sand for the heat to absorb.

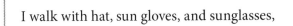

I walk with hat, sun gloves, and sunglasses,

With cell phone and bottle of water in hand,

Admiring the flora and fauna of the land,

Beautiful blooming prickly pear and saguaro cactus.

I stop while perspiration runs down my back,

The air is hot; and like a hair dryer, the breeze.

I ask, "Am I in Tucson or am I in Hades?"

There's white salt stain on my shirt of black.

Desert flowers' fragrance fills the air,

Hummingbird goes for the nectar.

It's one hundred degrees and I'm a spectator

In June – the hottest month of the year.

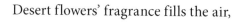

DNA Sidewalks

We don't want your DNA on our shoes and feet;

If you're spitting on sidewalks, please quit.

People walking down the sidewalks of concrete

Have to look down to dodge the spit.

Dogs on leash walk through the slime,

Then into your house and into your bed.

Instead of rest with peace of mind -

Count all the germs instead.

Goblet cells produce the phlegm,

Your throat wants to spit it up;

Spittoons are obnoxious and you can't find them;

Improvise with a tissue or small cup.

Your DNA should stay with you;

Be responsible outside your door.

You could try a dairy-free diet too.

As for mucous, less is more.

Please don't spit on the sidewalks,

In winter, I can slip on the "ice";

In summer, I might slip while wearing crocs,

Getting a concussion won't be nice.

Boomerang

I traveled to Australia,

    for tourist paraphernalia.

I bought a boomerang made of wood,

    symbolic of karma: bad or good.

What goes out always comes back

    just like a boomerang, on track.

II. Philosophy

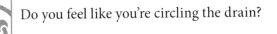

Circling the Drain

Do you feel like you're circling the drain?

Caught in a current? About to go down?

Feeling depression on the brain?

Is your heart heavy with smile changed to frown?

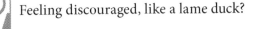

Feeling discouraged, like a lame duck?

Does it seem you're in quicksand, going down?

Do you feel lost, blaming all on bad luck?

Are you stuck?

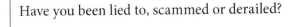

Have you been lied to, scammed or derailed?

In pain? As if smacked by a hockey puck?

Feeling frustrated that you've failed?

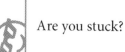

Are you stuck?

Feeling hopeless like a desperado?

After being struck by a truck?

Lying there motionless in the muck?

Are you stuck?

Go get unstuck.

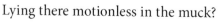

Look up, to the heavenly portal,

Ask for an anointing,

Claim a promise for a mortal:

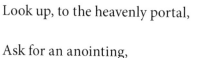

The Good News – John 3:16.

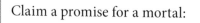

Get up on your feet and don't give up hope,

Rise up like a phoenix out of the fire,

Talk to someone, that will help you to cope,

Get out of the swamp and quagmire.

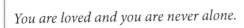

Jesus the Messiah stands at the door and knocks.

Revelation 3:20 (NIV)

You are loved and you are never alone.

You're unstuck, victorious – you've prevailed.

this and that

I asked, what is the definition of "this and that"?

Is it "this and that" or "that and this"?

Tell me – I need to know so I can put an end to what

Is so trivial but taking up valuable space.

"Various unspecified things" could be its focus,

Also "Miscellaneous to the nth degree",

"That" could be "far"; "this" could be "close",

It's all looking clearer to me.....

Talk is cheap.

Encouraging others is what will matter.

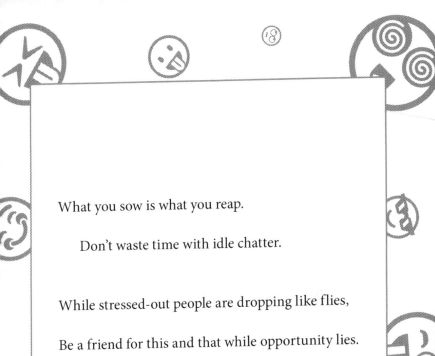

What you sow is what you reap.

Don't waste time with idle chatter.

While stressed-out people are dropping like flies,

Be a friend for this and that while opportunity lies.

Food Waster Over Water

A cruiser on a cruise ship elite

    Ate an entire fancy meal with dessert and wine,

Then requested something extra to eat,

    Took a bite and started to complain.

After complaining about a piece of meat,

    Cruiser left it on the plate,

Not hungry enough to eat,

    The wastage ending in a stalemate.

Food Waster On Land

You're at the dancehall in the middle of May,

But instead of cha-cha-cha and foxtrot,

You're obsessed with the buffet,

Circling the smorg while the food is hot.

There you go again, stimulated by food,

Piling high your plate with salads and fried chicken,

But only taking a bite or two, which is so rude,

And throwing half away with no inhibition.

What is the mindset behind the wasting?

Is it "extra pounds" off your waist?

Instead of wasting, you should be tasting,

And why dump the dessert? It's a disgrace.

You're taking too much and you want to grab.

Just think and have some self-control.

Take less if you want to lose your flab.

Don't pile high your plate and bowl.

Waltz, tango or line dance -

You haven't danced all night;

No calories burned – and no romance;

Just food wasted, so impolite.

III. Romance

ex-Harmony

I.

There was no harmony in our relationship. You were an online entity, then a voice over the phone. I knew there was no future for us. It was nice to get a text message from you once in a while. The e-mails you sent were interesting to read. But I didn't like how you asked for money "for groceries" for your "daughter" while you "were out of town".

You were taking up too much of my time on the phone. I could not proceed with my destiny. As Conway sings, it's only make believe. You need a reality check.

Adiós

II.

I can't believe I've received another e-mail from you, wanting more of my time. You're making my life too complicated.
There is no harmony in this online connection.

I'm hitting alt-control-delete.

Cad

You said I wasn't bad looking and you invited me to lunch.

Then you said you wanted to be more than just friends.

You said it was just a natural thing to get physical.

I've heard this non-committal point of view before.

I'm not in favor of this behavior (fornication).

I said it was a natural thing for married people.

Then you commented on how unattractive I look.

You don't look that great either – lacking hair, sometimes shaky.

Then you contacted me and told me not to contact you.

So, I went from being not bad looking to unattractive.

I think you've had too much sun.

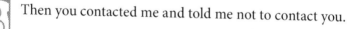

Friend

You're a shining star

    and I treasure our friendship.

We may not be soul mates

    but we have such a great rapport.

IV. Controversial

NOTE: This section only represents one point of view.
The next three poems may be offensive to some people.

Like the horror chambers in a wax museum, please
skip to the next section if you think you'll be offended.

Enter at your own risk.

Cross Dresser on a Cruise

You looked like a man when we met on Mardi Gras cruise --

Captivating smile and blue eyes, nice laugh.

Your voice was real high when you laughed, which amused --

But you looked good in your photograph.

Online you showed a different presence;

I recognized your face right away.

Wig, lipstick, jewelry, and female essence,

But your face still looked masculine, sad to say.

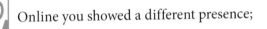

If you're born a man now why not just be a man?

Just live it out in stride.

Leave ladies' wigs and lipstick for women,

If you can't get a date – well then join pride.

LGBTQ

To all of you called LGBTQ,

    Why do you put this label on you?

The fancy title is over-rated;

    Why not keep life uncomplicated?

Two same-sex people – why not just be friends?

    You'll only be stuck in divorce when it ends,

Why marry (for insurance benefits?),

    And reap a bunch of regrets.

A man wants to be a woman – and now he is a she,

    A woman wants to be a man – and now she is a he,

The two trans people meet and marry in a ceremony

27

And start their new life as husband and wife or wife and husband.

In essence, men and women have both testosterone and estrogen,

Of course we could be attracted to both women and men,

If you're curious about same-sex attraction and a same-sex wife,

Leave it all in Vegas, but go on with a normal life: 1 man + 1 woman = married

Do it for the kids !

Living, growing, breathing, truthful, quintessential.

Mystery Man

When I first met you, you were a man.

Then you had surgery to become a woman.

Wig, lipstick, high heels, and skirt.

But you still have the bone structure of a man.

You look funny and you're not fooling anyone.

I hear that you still like girls.

I wish you wouldn't have had the surgery.

Why couldn't you just live it out?

Pat

Patricia wears a name badge that says "Pat."

At first glance, I thought she was a man.

Talk, clothes, and appearance were masculine.

Revealed by friends that, no, Pat is a woman!

I am relieved I did not try to flirt with Pat.

Change the name badge, please, to "Patricia."

It's only fair that people meet her as Patricia

And not as Patrick.

V. Work

Entrepreneur

I'll succeed and fail on my own terms.

And call myself an entrepreneur;

Avoiding life's tripping hazards and taking its turns,

Hoping I won't have to live in my car.

While other people are collecting welfare,

This S Corporation will join the team,

As a wage earning, tax paying solitaire,

Risking everything for the dream.

Words

Words in the form of a Christmas tree

    became a shape poem for all to see.

For humor, I added a limerick

    to make you want to dance a jig.

Some words spelled out a name to read

    becoming name or acrostic poetry.

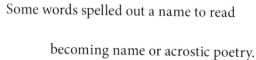

Prose did not rhyme and lacked formal meter;

    a natural flow of speech for the reader.

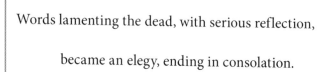

Words lamenting the dead, with serious reflection,

    became an elegy, ending in consolation.

Haiku, of three lines, made words come alive

      with five sound units, then seven, then five.

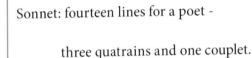

Sonnet: fourteen lines for a poet -

      three quatrains and one couplet.

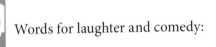

Words for laughter and comedy:

      humorous big, bad poetry.

I've written all these forms for you;

      I hope that you can use them too.

Sunburn

Bad sunburn on job

Help! Get me aloe vera

Painful lesson learned.

Max

Max lounged at home while the sun dipped low,

He sat down on the low, soft couch and

The couch was like a roasted marshmallow,

Swallowing him up like quicksand.

I tried helping him to a standing position

Pulling, pushing to escape the bondage;

I laughed out loud how gravity left him;

The couch was holding him hostage.

Fortunately a friendly local cop

Kindly stopped by to lend a hand;

He grabbed Max's hand and pulled him up;

Max walked away a free man.

Accolades to Max, who has a sense of humor,

At 94, walking, talking, thinking younger.

VI. Family

Mom

"Frieda loved to laugh."

This should have been your epitaph.

You enjoyed watching comedy shows

and laughed at the comedian on a cruise.

You laughed at the territorial family dog, Daisy,

and laughed when you sprayed Raid on your hair accidentally.

I'm glad I inherited your sense of humor on this journey,

Sharing big, bad laughter as it brings me to poetry.

I Hope I'm Not Being Disrespectful

I remember when we were together in the car --

   all of us talking and laughing as we drove.

It was the holidays and we had plans for family gathering,

   and it was such a pleasure to be back with each other again.

Then aunt had a senior moment and she

   couldn't remember what we were laughing about.

This just made everyone laugh even harder and louder.

   Totally unforgettable.

Regrets on the Shelf

Time passed so slow decades ago

And I squandered precious opportunity

To learn living as a family quid pro quo

But I chose frivolous friends over family.

My older sister wanted me to stop and play

But same-age school chums got in the way

Now my sister has passed away

And yesteryears' friends won't give me the time of day.

I wasn't present for you, sister.

I wasn't a support system for you, which you needed.

I didn't understand life.

Now I'm old and time passes by so fast

I remember a long time ago when you cried for a sister

I wish I could go back and re-live the past

To ease the pain I caused in us both to fester.

How do I add humor while day breaks,

When I have regrets on the shelf?

I say, learn from others' mistakes –

You don't have time to make them all yourself.

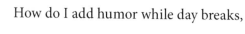

VII. Pets

Hobo

You were a stray cat, with black and white tuxedo coat.

Nice natured, too, and our family fed you along with our other cats.

I named you Hobo.

You had a cute name and people often smiled when you were mentioned.

Your name was Hobo, but you had a home – at our place.

And when you accidentally swallowed a small fish attached to a fishing line,

My brothers drove miles with you to a veterinarian to remove the hook.

Then the brothers brought you back home.

My Sister Helen

Helen cared for her pet goldfish with fond regard.

After the fish had swum their last she buried them,

Each with their own cross and grave in our backyard.

Helen adored her green parakeet named Greenie.

My sister was a gentle soul who connected with her pets.

When Helen was old enough to ride, she got a pony.

Daisy

You were our dog, living at our place

From a newborn pup's first breath

To a retired canine's death.

Known as "the daze",

You tried to keep all dogs away from our yard.

I remember how you would run real fast through the yard,

And then bark at any dogs in the distance.

If a dog would approach,

Your fur would stand up on the back of your neck.

You never ever hurt anyone.

You were just territorial, full of energy,

And you brought a lot of joy into our lives.

After you passed away, I saw a dog in our yard – and you were missed.

Chopper

Chopper was known as "Chopstix" at the cat shelter in Kodiak, where he was a resident for three years. He had been found wandering along a street before being rescued.

I adopted him and brought him to Anchorage, feeling fortunate that the condominium I owned, with all its rules, did allow pets. Chopper now had a pet guardian.

I decided to leave Alaska on a road trip in a Ford Explorer and drive to New York City, with a kennel in the back for Chopper. Our first night on the road presented a problem – there was one hotel in town but pets were not allowed. Service animals were allowed . . . at $100 a night. So Chopper remained cooped up that late May night because there was no service animal document.

Hospitality has been much better in other places. During the months since we left Anchorage, I found that some places accepted pets and some didn't. In Tucson, Chopper was allowed in a motel and apartment complex.

So many people are alone: no parents, no spouse, no children, and no siblings – so why aren't pets allowed?

Having a pet means you're not alone. Caring for a pet is therapeutic.

Loving a pet makes life worthwhile. Being loved by a pet – priceless!

Author's Note

After writing a cookbook, a book on travel, and two other books of a serious nature, I wanted to attempt poetry and share humor.

As a writer, I sincerely hope that *Big, Bad Poetry: Biggest and Baddest in the West* will give you a few laughs and brighten your day. Life is supposed to be happy and we should be encouraging each other.

As a Christian, I cannot pass up the opportunity to remind you to stop by your/a church and talk to a pastor. And choose Jesus of Nazareth as your Savior and ask Him to have Lordship of your life.

Choose Jesus –

> He is the way and the truth and the life. (John 14:6) (NIV)

> If you declare with your mouth, "Jesus is Lord," and believe in your heart that God raised him from the dead, you will be saved. (Romans 10:9) (NIV)

May your life be filled with joy, laughter, and faith!

Printed in the United States
By Bookmasters